Sacred
Actions
Journal

Cover and Interior Designed by Ashley Millhouse
All illustrations by Dana O'Driscoll
Type set in Grand Duke/Bressay

ISBN: 978-0-7643-6563-8
Printed in India

Published by REDFeather Mind, Body, Spirit
An imprint of Schiffer Publishing, Ltd.
4880 Lower Valley Road
Atglen, PA 19310
Phone: (610) 593-1777; Fax: (610) 593-2002
E-mail: Info@redfeathermbs.com
Web: www.redfeathermbs.com

For our complete selection of fine books on this and related subjects, please visit our website at www.redfeathermbs.com. You may also write for a free catalog.

REDFeather Mind, Body, Spirit's titles are available at special discounts for bulk purchases for sales promotions or premiums. Special editions, including personalized covers, corporate imprints, and excerpts, can be created in large quantities for special needs. For more information, contact the publisher.

We are always looking for people to write books on new and related subjects. If you have an idea for a book, please contact us at proposals@schifferbooks.com.

Sacred Actions Journal

A Wheel of the Year Journal for Sustainable and Spiritual Practices

Dana O'Driscoll

REDFeather™
MIND | BODY | SPIRIT

4880 Lower Valley Road, Atglen, PA 19310

Contents

To the White Burl Oak.

INTRODUCTION:
Sacred Actions and
the Wheel of the Year

In today's challenging times, those who practice any form of nature-based spirituality are often looking for ways to connect more deeply with the land and live in more intentional, meaningful ways. We recognize the considerable challenges before us, and we want to engage in actions that ensure that all life on this planet is protected for future generations. This journal is meant to help you more deeply attune to a wheel of the year practice focusing on sustainability, reflect on your own sacred actions and growing connection with the living earth, develop new meaningful journaling techniques, and ultimately, create a positive vision for the future. This is done through two concepts—the concept of sacred action and through the eight-fold Neopagan wheel of the year.

What Is Sacred Action?

"Sacred" is something that is connected, meaningful, reverent, and tied to our sense of the metaphysical or divine. Most of the time, this word is used to separate spiritual activity from mundane life: these are the special moments, ceremonies, or spiritual insights that impact us deeply. When we experience a sense of the sacred, it fills us with wonder, awe, and purpose. For those practicing nature spirituality or other earth-honoring activities like herbalism or permaculture, nature herself is considered sacred. "Action" implies doing something. It means that we offer our time, energy, and effort toward a goal. Thus, the idea of sacred action is extension and synthesis of these two definitions.

Sacred action is about us learning how to align our outer lives with our inner reverence for nature, and through doing so, allows us to make lifestyle changes that cultivate care for all beings and live in a way that heals and regenerates the living earth. Sacred action is about doing sustainable things in our own lives to honor the earth and lessen our burden upon her. It is through these seemingly mundane changes that we create a better today, a better tomorrow, and cultivate a vision for a better future for all life on this planet. These steps can be taken regardless of who we are, where we live, how many resources or supports we have, or any other aspects of our identities and lives. Thus, sacred action is about each of us working to make meaningful shifts in not only the way we think about the world but the impact of our specific actions in it.

Sacred action focuses on creating more connected, reverent, and holistic lives. I think a lot of us fear for the future–for our world, for our families, for our young, for this planet and all life on it. Engaging in sacred actions is a meaningful and powerful way of helping us move forward to more sustainable and grounded lives in the present and creating a powerful vision for the future. *Sacred Actions* draws upon a host of related areas including permaculture design, herbalism, sustainable living, regenerative agriculture, reskilling, the slow movement, local foods, organic gardening, and many more.

Sacred Actions follows a Wheel of the Year Approach to allow you to focus on creating sustainable and sacred practices tied to different aspects of daily life through the eight-fold wheel of the year. Sacred actions includes both inner and outer practices. We begin by considering the role of caring for the earth, each other, and ourselves as well as building our knowledge and skills through reskilling. In later chapters, we turn our attention to our consumption, our homes, our food, our yards and outdoor spaces, our communities, and the spiritual tools we use in the world. In this journal, sections are dedicated to each of these topics, with prompts, activities, and information to help you reflect upon your own goals and practices of sacred action. Prompts focus on both helping you deeply understand yourself and cultivate mindsets for this work. Activities help guide you during each of the eight stations of the year to deepen your own sacred action and sustainable practices.

How to Use This Journal

The *Sacred Actions Journal* that you are holding is a companion to *Sacred Actions: Living the Wheel of the Year through Earth-Centered Sustainable Practices* (REDFeather, 2021). You can use the journal in conjunction with the *Sacred Actions* book or use it independently. You can also choose to start this journal at any point on the wheel of the year, or you may choose to start this at the Winter Solstice, at the very beginning. Either use allows you a way of reflecting on the practice of sustainable spirituality and aligning your inner spiritual principles with your outer actions.

Each of the eight sections has an overview that offers insights into the theme for that station on the Wheel of the Year. Each of the eight sections of the wheel include 10–15 prompts for journaling and meditation, 5–8 sacred actions activities, and a creative journaling practice. Each creative journaling practice offers you a different approach to use writing and reflective activity to deepen your understanding and support your sacred actions in the world. In addition to the prompts, each section offers blank journal pages, which can be used to record your own sacred actions journey.

Keeping a Sacred Journal

Journaling is a way to record and document your path, reflect upon your experience, gain deeper insight about yourself and the world around you, express your creativity, and deeply engage with your own sacred work in the world. Writing is a very powerful activity that can deepen your practice and allow you to understand yourself in new ways.

Several key benefits exist for keeping a journal about your spiritual practices as they relate to sacred action. Sacred actions are things you do to align your inner spirituality and outer reality. That work is fun, engaging, and sometimes difficult—and it puts you in a space of living your practice. Journaling allows you to step back from that practice and take time to understand it, and how that practice is shaping you within or without. As you'll experience with the journaling strategies in each of the chapters in the *Sacred Actions Journal*, you can gain great spiritual benefit from journaling: getting into a flow state, engaging with your journals creatively, enhancing your learning, gaining deeper awareness, and even, visioning the future. Whether you are new to a sacred journaling practice or whether you've done journaling before, writing about your experience can be a powerful catalyst for even further growth. The following are some basic guidelines for keeping your *Sacred Actions Journal* and for a general journaling practice.

Create a regular writing practice. As with any other set of spiritual practices, the most effective spiritual journals are those that we keep with some regularity. Regular writing might mean once a week for some people or once a day for others. Still others may write when they have an experience that warrants it (which could average to once or twice a month). The important thing is not how often you write, but that you do write and make it part of your regular life.

Write as soon as you can after an experience. When you have meaningful spiritual experiences, such as through doing the rituals and practices in *Sacred Actions*, you should write them down as soon as possible. This is because when we are in the immediacy of an experience, we have one set of thoughts, emotions, and understandings. You will remember the key details. As time passes, our understanding of the experience shifts as we share the story with others or reflect back. Thus, if you reflect on an experience from a few days ago, the insights you may have will be different than if you write about it immediately.

Write to your future self, to tell a story and keep a record. It is helpful to record what you are thinking and feeling in the moment in enough detail that the journal entry will make sense to you later. All journaling is storytelling; in the case of your journal, you are telling a story to your future self.

Allow yourself to expand beyond the experience. In the process of telling a story, our understanding of it deepens and grows. Thus, journaling is not just a process of writing down exactly what happened or what the insights were, but it's also a powerful tool and opportunity to ponder or sit with those experiences further. Thus, as you are writing, allow yourself to process the experience, noting any deeper insights or awarenesses that come from the act of writing. Ask yourself questions and leave notes for your future self to consider.

Have tools that you enjoy using. It is an excellent idea to set yourself up for enjoyment with your journaling practice. One of the ways to do that is make sure you have the tools that bring you joy: pens, papers, inks, and anything else that allows you to create an enjoyable experience.

Establish rituals. Writing rituals help you get in the mood and habit of writing, these are activities that help prepare the mind and body for your sacred journaling practice. This can include almost anything: brewing up a cup of your favorite tea, sitting in your favorite spot, playing certain music, smoke cleansing yourself and your journal, etc. Consider if there are sacred rituals you want to do—like a protection or grounding—before you sit down to write. For example, you might do deep breathing, smoke cleansing, and then light a candle before sitting down to write.

Consider other reflective methods. Some people have difficulty keeping a regular journal or sitting down to write. If this is the case for you, you might consider an alternative method—speaking into a recording device and transcribing what you have written later is one method that works. This method still allows you to gain the reflective and storytelling benefits of journaling. You might also use meditation practices to first reflect upon your responses to the various prompts and then write down the most important concepts. Other reflective practices are detailed more in the sections of this journal.

CHAPTER 1

Winter Solstice:
The Ethics of Care

The Sacred Actions Wheel of the Year begins at the Winter Solstice, when the earth is plunged into darkness, the sun hangs low in the sky, and it feels like all hope has been lost. But the Winter Solstice is also a time when we honor the return of the light, when we overcome the darkness, and when the seeds of hope are planted. Many people today, including those who practice earth-based spirituality, are fearful of the coming darkness, fearful of how our planet will fare in the coming decades or centuries, and pray for a new path for humanity. That path is ultimately rooted in care and a desire to reconnect with the living earth. If we as individuals and communities can build care back into our conversations, our decisions, our governance, and our cultures, then philosophies of care and nurturing—rather than those of profit and exploitation—can start to drive our decisions and actions as a species.

Using permaculture's ethics system as a guiding philosophy, we can see that care has multiple aspects: caring for earth and all her inhabitants, caring for humanity in all varied forms, and only taking our fair share, that others may live in abundance. Earth care can include activities to reduce our ecological footprint and our burden upon the land, and it can include regenerative activities like planting gardens, replacing lawns, and doing conservation work. People care can include community-oriented activity, such as organizing spaces for people to meet and share, teaching others, and finding ways of helping heal and nurture those in your immediate life. Fair share focuses on how we can monitor our own consumption and waste and turn our waste into resources that are used and cycled. It reminds us that everything we consume ultimately is taken from the living earth, and thus, we can be careful about what we consume, how much we consume, and how resources can be gently returned after use. A final consideration is self-care—how we care for ourselves so that we can do our broader work in the world. By bringing care back into the forefront of our conversations and making care a core value in our lives, we can begin to create a new vision—a hopeful vision—for future generations.

Prompts for Meditation and Journaling

1. What does the word "care" mean to you?
2. What are activities that you already do to cultivate care in your life? What are activities you would like to do?
3. Consider making a list of activities that you consider nurturing vs. those that are considered exploitative in our broader culture. How might you personally work towards supporting care-oriented activities?
4. What does "earth care" mean to you? How might you manifest this in your life? What do you already do to engage in earth care?
5. What does "people care" mean to you? How might you manifest this in your life? What do you already do to engage in people care?
6. What does "fair share" mean to you? How might you manifest this in your life? What do you do already to engage in people care?
7. Tell a story of your own local community and how it might be different using care-oriented philosophies rather than profit-oriented ones. What would change?
8. How do you think we can encourage others to embrace an ethics of care? What would that look like? What could that do to our world?
9. Consider the concept of empathy as it applies to all life. What does an empathic approach look like?
10. Share your own story of a time that you acted in a very care-oriented way. Reflect on what this taught you about yourself and the care you offer others.
11. Reflect on your own practice of self-care (if you have one). What do you do well?
12. Do you ever prevent yourself from engaging in self-care? What is the root of this action and how might you change it?
13. What does the darkness at the winter solstice symbolize for you?
14. When does the return of the light at the winter solstice symbolize for you?
15. Reflect upon others in your life who have shown you deep care. How did their actions affect you?

Sacred Actions: Experiences and Activities

1. Spend time listening to the stories and wisdom of someone that you believe lives in a care-oriented way. Learn what you can from this person, not only about what they do now, but their journey to bring this philosophy into their lives. Consider what you take away from this conversation and how it may shape your own story moving forward.

2. Consider one way that you can engage in earth care, where you care directly for the land and beings who live in the land. Enact this in your life and reflect on the results.

3. Consider one way that you can engage in people care, where you work to care for others in your local environment. Enact this in your life and reflect on the results.

4. Consider one way that you can engage in fair share, where you reduce your consumption and use only what you need. Enact this in your life and reflect on the results.

5. At the time of darkness on the land, spend some time in full darkness or only with the light of the moon. What does this teach you about the wheel of the year and sacred action?

6. At this time of darkness, spend an evening living by candlelight, slowing down, and simply being present with the darkness of this time of year. What did you learn from this experience?

Journaling Strategy: Personal Storytelling

When we first have an experience, there is an immediacy to it as we are immersed in the sensory journey of that moment. But as time passes, we can develop deeper and layered relationships with that experience and consider the experience from multiple angles. One of the ways of exploring experiences in more depth is through writing, where we reflect and consider new angles, and our understanding deepens and expands.

This concept of deep learning through our writing is directly tied to the ancient art of storytelling. Storytelling, an integral part of the human experience, allows us to go deeper with each retelling, to consider new angles when others respond and share. You might consider your journal like a story you are writing to your future self. Here are some strategies for this journaling approach:

» *Start by seeing your journal as an opportunity to tell your future self a story.* Since the only person who will read it is your future self, tell yourself your story.

» *Create space for you to write and process about experiences.* Just allow yourself to follow whatever leads or threads you may want to and allow the words to flow. Don't worry about the grammar, spelling or sentence structure—just let the words flow.

» *Consider how the specific experience you are writing about lends you deeper insight into more general areas: the patterns of your life, aspects of yourself or your identity, or your future goals.* Often, when we compare specific experiences to broader patterns, they can teach us a great deal about who we are.

» *Use a series of writing techniques over time to delve deeply into your most powerful experiences.*
  » *First, do what you can to write about the experience in the moment— try to capture it as soon as possible.* Consider your audience for this experience your future self. If you do not have your journal available, one technique is to use a voice recorder to record you sharing the story or experience with your future self. For particularly powerful experiences, it is better to capture the details in the moment and not worry if the journal entry is well written.
  » *After a few days with the experience, return to your journal and tell the story a second time.* Again, write to your future self about the experience. How does this retelling offer you more insight?
  » *After some time has passed, re-read your first two entries about the experience and if you feel led, write again.*
  » *Simply create space for you to reflect or process it.*
» *Work to get into the "flow" of your writing (see Ch.* 5 Summer Solstice for more on this concept).
» *Allow yourself to return to your writing over time, retelling yourself stories, looking for patterns, and understanding new connections (see Ch.* 8 Samhain for more on this concept).

CHAPTER 2

Imbolc:
Wisdom through Oak Knowledge and Reskilling

We move through the Wheel of the Year to Imbolc, which for many in temperate climates, is still a time of darkness and cold upon the land. This is a time when we turn inward and use this time for reflection, study, and practice. In our Sacred Actions Wheel of the Year, Imbolc focuses on building knowledge and learning new skills and practices.

In the modern era, we have lost many traditional skills that our ancestors would have practiced, many of which allow for more sustainable living. The concept of "oak knowledge" comes from the word "druid" which, for the ancient druids, meant knowledge of the oaks. Many ancient peoples were acorn eating cultures, where knowledge of the oaks would have allowed them to process acorns into food, use oak wood to build shelters and heat their homes, and practice interdependence in their immediate landscapes. A more modern term, reskilling, is another way to think about gaining knowledge. Reskilling is a global movement that covers a wide range of traditional skills and crafts that our ancestors would have had, but that many of us have lost due to modern life. Our grandparents and great grandparents held these skills, but they were not passed on.

These are skills that include taking care of our basic needs: fermentation and traditional food preservation, gardening, animal husbandry, spinning, weaving, and learning how to create our own clothes. These skills also include making functional items for daily life: sewing, wood carving, natural building, blacksmithing, and other traditional crafts. Oak knowledge may also include deeper awareness and knowledge of nature: how to use plants, trees, and other parts of nature for food, shelter, medicine, clothing, and more. Any of these skills allows you to create things directly from the land around you, which allows you to control the means of harvest, production, and use to ensure an equitable and sustainable harvest. This is opposed to purchasing products whose origins—and thus, environmental impact—may be unknown.

The point of all of this is simple: the more that we can learn to provide at least some of our own needs using resources that we can gather ourselves or gain locally, the more sustainably we can live and the more we can empower ourselves to live in a care-oriented and regenerative way on our great earth. Further, the practice of these traditional skills can bring you close to nature and to your own creative gifts, which has a host of spiritual benefits. Building oak knowledge and reskilling also allows you to cultivate a more reciprocal and gratitude-filled relationship with the land outside of your door.

Prompts for Meditation and Journaling

1. Consider something that you've always wanted to learn. What is it? Why are you drawn to learning it?

2. Following up, now consider how you might learn this skill. Who are the people who could teach you? Where might this knowledge be found? What are the tools or steps involved?

3. Psychologist Howard Gardener's theory of multiple intelligences suggests that people have at least eight different kinds of intelligences. Traditional book learning would include logical-mathematical intelligence and linguistic-verbal intelligence. Other intelligences include interpersonal (understanding the actions and emotions of people), intrapersonal (being aware of your own emotional state), musical, bodily-kinesthetic (which would include movement and dance), visual-spatial (visualizing, observing, maps, and graphics), and naturalistic (knowledge of nature). Based on this list, which kinds of intelligence do you already feel you have? Which would you like to grow further?

4. Reflect on a skill that your grandparents or great grandparents had that was not passed on. What was it? What meaning does it hold for you now?

5. Creativity is a big part of building and applying new knowledge. How do you cultivate creativity in your life? How might you bring more creativity in?

6. Reskilling is often an embodied activity. Consider your own body as a tool for learning. What does your body do well? What does it offer you?

7. Consider how where you live determines what you learn. What are some unique things that you know because of where you live? What are local teachers or schools you might go to learn?

8. What does the term "oak knowledge" mean to you?

9. Reflect on the person who you consider the best teacher or mentor that you've had. Who was this person and what did they teach you?

10. How do you see reskilling and building oak knowledge as a spiritual practice?

11. Reflect upon your ancestors—more recent or more ancient. We have many different kinds of ancestors: those of blood, of land, of tradition, and of craft/profession. Which ancestors are you drawn to and why? How might you honor them?

12. How do you learn best? What creates an enjoyable learning experience for you? How might you draw upon that for reskilling?

Sacred Actions: Experiences and Activities

1. Find someone who is much older than you and ask them to teach you something. Reflect on the experience.

2. Find someone who is much younger than you and ask them to teach you something. Reflect on the experience and, if you also did the first activity, consider the difference between these two areas.

3. Go visit a museum of history or a living history fair and look at the tools and objects from ages past. What are you drawn to? Do you see anything that you could try to make and use?

4. Map out your current set of skills that can provide your basic needs and help you navigate the world (clothing, food, shelter, everyday uses, interpersonal skills). After you map out your list, reflect on it.

5. Map out your "dream" list of skills and oak knowledge. What do you want to learn or wish you knew? How might you get there?

6. Learn something about your ancient human ancestors. How did they live? Where did they live? What foods sustained them? Consider if any of their ancient wisdom may be applied to your present life.

7. Learn something about the pre-industrial human ancestors where you live. How did they live? What kinds of shelter did they use? What can they teach you?

Journaling Strategy: Writing to Learn and Grow

One of the foundational understandings about writing is that it's a tool—a tool that humans have created over time to help them process and learn. Writing helps us learn by allowing us to reflect upon what we already know and write our way into deeper understanding about the world around us. This is particularly useful when we think about the kinds of things writing can help us do at Imbolc: reskilling is all about learning and integrating that learning into our beings.

In the field of Writing Studies, this concept is called "writing to learn"—the idea that writing can facilitate our own deep growth process and understanding. That is, while we can read, attend classes, and apply our learning in new ways, if we write about it, we can gain even deeper insight in ways no other tool gives us. This deep insight can come about not only through note taking or other forms of writing for the purposes of memory, but also through simply reflecting on the process. Here are some tips to facilitate writing to learn and grow in your spiritual journaling practice:

» *Write to learn more deeply.* Many people don't feel they fully understand something till they try to write about it. Thus, spend time writing about the things you are learning and see what deep insights arise.

» *Note taking.* Your journal can be an opportunity to take notes on things that you are very excited to learn and want to remember. For this, consider combining note taking strategies with idea generation strategies (see Ch. 4 Beltane) and visual journaling (see Ch. 6 Lughnassadh).

» *The KWL activity.* One practice that facilitates deep learning of this is to ask three interrelated questions: What do I know already? What do I want to learn? And after you've learned something, reflect on: What did I learn and how can I put that into practice?

» *Write to share with others.* One of the best ways of mastering new learning is to share it with others. Consider writing something small that can be shared with others on your learning journey such as through a blog or short article.

» *Make plans for integrating learning and life.* A journal is a great place to consider how what you are learning can apply to your life in a direct way. What does your specific sacred action in the world look like? How might it be unique to you, to your circumstances, and to your strengths?

CHAPTER 3

Spring Equinox:
Spring Cleaning and Disposing of the Disposable Mindset

A t the Spring Equinox, the tradition of "spring cleanup" and cleansing of the home and hearth is present. While in traditional times, spring cleaning mean that the house would be aired out and cleaned, in the 21st century, this tradition often shifts to one of decluttering and getting rid of excess stuff. But if we look at those living in more traditional cultures or look at nature herself—there is no waste. Everything that is used is re-used again and again, with perfect recycling systems. It is only in the modern age that we have generated enormous amounts of waste and garbage—and these are polluting our world and leaving a terrible legacy for generations to come. Hence, the theme of our Sacred Actions Wheel of the Year at the Spring Equinox is "disposing of the disposable mindset" and looking for ways to reduce, reuse, and recycle. To live in care and harmony with the living earth, we need to learn to reject the materialist lifestyle, learn to live in a way where we only take what we need to survive, and learn how to turn waste into a resource.

The work of the Spring Equinox has several different dimensions including considering the inner and outer problems of waste and how to address the enormous amount of excess "stuff" that seems to flow into our lives. We can consider the "inner" problem of waste, and how a waste-filled life and world has implications for our own mental health and spiritual well-being. Towards practical approaches to eliminating waste and excess stuff, we might look to a host of waste monitoring strategies such as shifting our practices away from disposable products, addressing excess spending and consumption, and work to reduce our own ecological footprint. We also have a range of possibilities for taking personal responsibility for our own waste: addressing plastic waste through ecobricks (where you create building blocks from non-recyclable plastic), learning how to repurpose and re-use our own and others' waste, learning composting and vermicomposting, and learning how to recycle our own human waste through producing humanure and liquid gold. All these approaches help us start to live waste-free lives and put us much more deeply in tune with the living earth. While these practices are certainly challenges in a culture that is designed to produce waste, they are well worth pursuing.

Prompts for Meditation and Journaling

1. If you were going to downsize into a studio apartment and/or tiny house, what of your current possessions would you keep? After you've made this list, reflect on it. How does that show you what you value in terms of material possessions?

2. Consider what is truly important to you in your life. Make a list and then reflect on it. How does this relate to your own waste and consumption?

3. Consider the terms "garbage," "junk," and/or "waste" and reflect on your cultural understanding of these terms. How do language labels impact how we see the world? What if we re-labeled "waste" as "resource"?

4. Meditate on one object in your life that has meaning to you. Reflect on its story and its full cycle of production and consumption—the raw materials that came from the earth to make this object; how it was made, packaged, and transported; and what might happen after it leaves your life. How long will it take to return to the earth in any form? What does this teach you?

5. As a follow-up, now consider this same object from the perspective of the raw materials and object itself and tell the object's story from a first-person perspective (e.g., if it contains wood, consider the perspective of the tree). How does this change your viewpoint?

6. Consider the cultural conditioning you have concerning waste, consumption, and materialism. These are things we assume, automatic behaviors we engage in, or practices that we don't always question (e.g., putting trash on the curb). How are you addressing this cultural conditioning? What might you do next?

7. Now, imagine you are one of your ancient ancestors in a hunter-gatherer society and write about modern culture from their perspective. What would they see and experience?

8. Consider the difference between staying in a cluttered, dirty place vs. a clean and open place. What does this do to your mental and spiritual senses?

9. Compile a list of your needs vs. your wants. Reflect on these and consider items for action.

10. Consider the non-material things that you consume. Reflect on how this consumption makes you feel, and what it does to your life.

11. How do the concepts of people care, earth care, and fair share tie to the concept of waste and materialism?

Sacred Actions: Experiences and Activities

1. Go "waste free" for one week (or if you want a real challenge, one month). What does it take to accomplish this? Is it possible? How do you feel afterwards?

2. Because less than 1% of what is produced and consumed is in circulation less than six months later, one of the challenges we have is making sure that what we buy will last. Make a commitment to eliminate at least one waste stream in your life by transitioning to something that will last (e.g., investing in cast iron cookware). Then, reflect on this change in your journal.

3. Explore options for composting and choose an option that works for you. What might you be able to do? (E.g., urban dwellers can join a compost co-op or learn vermicomposting, while suburban dwellers might opt for a compost tumbler or traditional compost pile.)

4. Save something you would typically throw away. Find a way to give this item a second life or purpose. Reflect on this experience.

5. Spend time observing waste streams in your home or work life. First, reflect on what they currently are and document them. Then, consider what you might do to reduce or eliminate one waste stream.

6. Save all your unrecyclable plastic for one month. How much is there? Consider making an ecobrick and/or finding another use for this material.

Journaling Strategy: Perspective Journaling

The Spring Equinox is a good time to consider how our cultural conditioning may set us up for behaviors and activities that are not in line with our ethical principles. One strategy for doing this, reflected in some of the above prompts, is to do so through the creative approach of writing from perspectives that are different than our own. Perspective journaling allows you to build care and empathy into your daily interactions and really consider the world from multiple angles.

The practice is simple: select a different perspective to take and write from that perspective. Write from the perspective, for example, of a tree along your city street, a disposable cup, a person who lives in a different part of the world from you, your ancient ancestor, a person of the future who is not yet born, or of the stream that flows through your city. Consider what perspective you might want to take and how it will help you in your path towards sacred actions. Once you've written from this perspective, respond from your own perspective. How does the words of someone from a different perspective shape, deepen, or change your perspective? Consider also how this practice may be useful in helping you "dispose of the disposable mindset" with regards to materialism and consumerism.

CHAPTER 4
Beltane:
Sacred Actions in Our Homes

Sacred Action at Beltane focuses on our immediate homes and everyday lives. The home is our center of our world, it is the place where we feel most at ease, the place where we have the most control, and the place where we spend much of our time. Thus, it is a perfect place for us to make meaningful, sustainable changes. One of the approaches to enacting sacred action within our lives is by seeing our homes as a sacred space and thus, by considering how we can engage in sacred activities that enrich our homes and honor the living earth.

These activities are quite wide ranging and cover many aspects of our daily lives. In the kitchen, we can think about alternative methods for cooking our food, such as learning how to cook using solar cookers, hayboxes, Dutch ovens, hearth cooking, and other older—yet more sustainable technologies. We can consider more sustainable alternatives for heating, such as rocket mass heaters, wood cookstoves, being strategic with using shade and the sun, and being selective about how and when we heat our homes. We can consider our water usage—how to create greywater systems, how to harvest water from our roofs, and how to employ water-sinking features in our yards and gardens like swales and rain gardens. When we clean, we can create our own cleaning supplies, such as soaps, laundry detergents, and cleaners from simpler, safe ingredients that can replace waterway-damaging commercial products. We can reconsider how we use lighting at night and slow down with candlelight living. Finally, we can consider more radical shifts, such as tiny house living, downsizing, and other ways of reducing our ecological footprint. These kinds of activities can all bring us in line with the living earth and jump start our sacred action in the world in powerful ways.

Prompts for Meditation and Journaling

1. Reflect on your home as a sacred space. In what ways have you already made it a sacred space? In what directions might you want to move to continue to do so?

2. Reflect on the relationship between the terms "sacred" and "space." How do these two come into relationship for you?

3. Consider your daily life and walk through the typical actions of your day. Where might you build in moments of sacred activity? What benefits could this have for you?

4. Create a mindmap of all the normal activities and consumption activities of your home. Once you've created your map, reflect on how you might intervene—where is a good place to start?

5. Reflect on the waterways in your area. What does clean water mean to you? How might you protect it? Where does your water come from?

6. Consider your ideal living circumstances and ideal home. Write about it in as much vivid detail as you can.

7. Tell the story of your home and life five years from now, after you've put some of the principles of sacred action in place (see visioning, Ch. 8 Samhain).

8. After telling this story, create a plan to help you achieve this, one step at a time. How does it feel to create such a plan?

9. Consider the things that most bring you joy in your home. What are they? How might these be tied to sacred action?

10. How might you talk to family members, roommates, or guests about the home as a sacred space?

11. How can you bring the sacred into everyday life?

Sacred Actions: Experiences and Activities

1. Learn one alternative cooking method, such as using a haybox, building and using a simple rocket stove or solar cooker, replacing regular pots and pans with indestructible cast iron, or experimenting with Dutch oven cooking. How does changing your cooking method change your relationship with your time and your food?

2. Spend some time in "earth time" or "slow time." This is a time without clocks, without to-do lists, without a cell phone and notifications. What do you gain from this experience?

3. Try to visit an ecovillage or other place that has some of the sustainable technologies associated with everyday living. What did you learn from this visit? How did using these technologies—as opposed to contemporary ones—make you feel?

4. Explore and enact one water catchment (rain barrel, rain garden, swale) or water recycling method (greywater). What does this teach you about the value of clean water?

5. If you live with others, have a conversation with other family members / roommates in your home about sustainable practices. See what the group can agree to do and move forward in sacred action and in community.

6. Learn more about your human ancestors and their everyday lives and living. Find one thing you can integrate into your own life that would honor them and their ways in your home.

Journaling Strategy: Idea Generation through Mindmapping, Freewriting, and Free Association

We can use writing to cultivate our creativity and idea generation, or what the ancient Greeks called "invention." Invention strategies are those that allow you to both take stock in what you already know and creatively generate new ideas that you can put to use towards sacred action. Thus, we will explore a triad of techniques that you can use, not only in integrating sustainable practices into your home life at Beltane, but also throughout the year. Idea generation techniques work, in part, because they tap into your subconscious and also help you generate a deeper understanding. They are a way for you to simply put down everything you know and later, return to your idea generation and continue to build.

Mindmapping. Mindmapping is creating a set of associations and bubbles on a central theme. The central theme can be anything that you are working toward, such as "sustainability in the kitchen." Placing that theme in the center, you then work off of the theme to see how many circles you can connect to them. Any number of circles can branch off from any of the nodes—and eventually you get something that looks like a web of associations and connections.

Freewriting. With freewriting, you choose a theme and then allow yourself to write freely, not paying attention to sentence structure, grammar, spelling, coherence, or any other issues. With freewriting, you just allow anything that you want to write to come to the surface and write. If you type quickly, you might be able to keep up with your thoughts faster using typing than handwriting. You can use freewriting for any of the prompts in this journal.

Free Association. Free association is like freewriting except that it is not in paragraph form. In this technique, you allow content from your subconscious to rise to the surface by expressing whatever thoughts and feelings come to you without judgement or reserve. List terms and see what comes to you as you explore them. Free association can be particularly good for processing challenging issues surrounding problematic culturally-oriented ideologies as well as understanding our own selves deeper from within.

CHAPTER 5

Summer Solstice: Sacred Food and Nourishment

The Summer Solstice is when the summer's bounty of the gardens, fields, and forests begins to flow in. This is a perfect time to consider how food and nourishment can be a wonderful focus for sacred action and one that is very accessible to many people. Everyone has to eat, and every choice we make about the food that we bring into our lives and bodies is an opportunity to choose earth-honoring, sustainable, and sacred choices. Sacred actions within the realm of food has at least three different focuses: considering local and sustainable sourcing of as many foods as possible, eating by what is in season and abundant (including learning some wild food foraging), and honoring the lives that are given in the food you are eating.

On local foods, many places now have easy access to farmer's markets, farms that sell food, community gardens, food co-ops, our own gardens, or other ways of accessing local foods. Always check to ensure that your local farmers are engaging in sustainable methods for raising/growing food (e.g., chemical free, certified naturally grown, organic) and if they aren't already, encourage them to do so. Farmer's markets can produce so many good foods that you can build into your local diet. You might also want to start wild food foraging—foraging can take place even in urban areas, and can be a wonderful way to align with the seasons and the bounty of nature. For wild food foraging, make sure you are engaging in ethical practices: stick to plants that are abundant and not endangered, take only what you need, and ask permission and offer gratitude for what you take. If you do the above, you'll be eating in alignment with the seasons, and this will bring you into a deep place of sacred action.

Regardless of what you have access to, consider how you can build deep gratitude, care, and blessings into your relationship with food. Consider developing rituals for eating and offering gratitude to your food and the hands that prepare it: prayers at meals, wassailing rituals for the abundance and health of the land, and gratitude practices for the lives given (plant or animal).

Prompts for Meditation and Journaling

1. If you could be any fruit or vegetable, what would you be? Why?
2. Reflecting on your response above, what did you learn about yourself and your own connection to food through this? What are your values and/or things you care about?
3. Tell the story of the most meaningful or impactful meal you ever ate, the meal that sticks in your mind. What about it made it so impactful? Could you recreate this meal sustainably (if it wasn't already)? Why or why not?
4. Now, tell the story of a perfect future meal in your life. What would be on the menu? Who would you share it with? What makes that meal so special?
5. Food is often connected to our ancestors and customs. What foods were most important to your own ancestors? How might you create dishes that honor them?
6. Food also has deep regional connections. What is some of your favorite regional cuisine? What is the history of that cuisine? How are you personally connected to it? What is unique about your ecosystem that allows for special ingredients in this dish?
7. Make a list of what you would consider "healing foods" for your body. What do you feel when you eat them? How can you ensure these foods are local and sustainable?
8. Using mindmapping (see Ch. 4 Beltane) and make a mind map of the foods you regularly eat and their sources. What can you find local equivalents of?
9. You'll notice that many of the prompts above put you and your food in a care-based and ethics-based relationship. This is intentional—when we see our food (or any other aspect of our lives) in a care-oriented way, we make different choices. Reflect on the relationship of care—people care, earth care, and fair share—with your food. How does this change your relationship?
10. Have you found food in the wild? What was it and how did it taste? How did it make you feel? If you haven't, consider doing so!

Sacred Actions: Experiences and Activities

1. Wild food foraging can be an incredible experience when practiced sustainably and ethically. Learn to forage at least one wild food and cook that food into a meal.

2. Along with wild food foraging, learn what invasive species are also edible, and make it a point to harvest and prepare them. This does double duty—it allows you to help control the spread of invasive species and also enjoy a local meal.

3. Create an entirely local meal—visit a farmer's market, harvest from your garden, or go foraging and use only what you have gotten locally in a meal. What are the flavors and textures of that meal? How does that meal make you feel? How is it energetically different from what you might purchase at the store?

4. Learn an alternative food preservation method like canning, dehydrating, fermenting, smoking, or salting. How does this process and this food make an impact on your life?

5. Develop a small ritual surrounding your food—a gratitude, a blessing, an offering. How does this ritual shift your experience of eating?

6. Deep gratitude practices are those where you honor not only the food you are eating but the land that sustained it, the hands that grew it, packaged it, sold it, and prepared it. At each meal, offer your own sense of deep gratitude for these things. Practice deep gratitude for your food for a week and then reflect on this experience.

Journaling Strategy: Flow Writing

Flow is a word that describes a deep state of focus, meditation, and getting into "the zone" where you are fully invested in an activity. When you are in a flow state, you become deeply immersed in your work, you may lose track of time, and you may come out of the work with a sense of peace and tranquility. Anyone can cultivate a flow state in their lives. Psychologists who have studied the flow state recognize that it has similar benefits to meditation. Flow has deep spiritual connections as well. In the druid tradition, the Awen (symbol below) is also known as "flowing inspiration" and is seen as the inspiration that comes from divinity—either deity, the universe, or nature herself. The flow state, in this sense, can be part of a spiritual activity designed to put you deeper in connection with the living earth and the cosmos.

Flow is commonly associated with the act of writing, and many writers work to cultivate flow states as they find it allows them to uncover deeper insights, experience intrinsic joy in their writing, and write more often. Flow states are not just for writers but can occur in many aspects of our lives: in a variety of creative practices such as fine arts or crafts, song or playing music, dance or other movement, and storytelling. Flow can also enter our lives when we are engaged in aspects of our work or home lives—including when we are in the kitchen or garden. Flow is most recognized as something tied to creative and skilled practice, and thus, it is a wonderful thing to cultivate as part of a sacred journaling experience. Cultivating a flow state in your own journaling practice can open you up to deeper understandings.

Here are tips for cultivating a flow state in your writing:

» *Cultivate a regular journaling practice.* Flow states can be cultivated, in part, by regular practice. The more opportunities you create to experience flow, the more of a regular part of your life they will be. Thus, creating a daily or weekly journal practice can help you get into the flow in a regular way!

» *Find quiet time to write.* Flow states are about deep focus, which requires you to avoid distractions as much as possible when you are writing or creating. Thus, finding a quiet time of day, away from social media, family, pets, or other distractions will be most helpful to get you into the flow.

» *Use music, ambience, and ritual tools.* Find things that help set the stage for your journaling practice can help you experience flow.

» *Relax your body.* Before you sit down to write, do some stretching, movement, or any other relaxation to help you fully settle into the space.

» *Relax your mind.* Start with some deep breathing to help you settle into your writing practice. Focus on your breath and allow the other concerns of the world to drift away. Be with your writing, your journal, in this sacred space and time.

» *Ritually invite the **Awen** into your space.* In the druid tradition, druids often invite the flow of Awen into their lives by either using the symbol of the Awen or chanting the word drawn out (*Ah-oh-en*). You can keep an Awen symbol near your journal or use the chant to bring in the flow.

CHAPTER 6

Lughnassadh: Landscapes, Gardens, Wildtending, and Lawn Liberations

I n the Sacred Actions Wheel of the Year, Lughnassadh is the season of the first harvest, and thus, it is an excellent time of year to harvest from an existing garden and start to plan a garden for the following year. Many people start gardens because of what we can harvest from them: food, medicine, and ritual supplies (like growing plants for smoke clearing sticks and incense). But gardens have so many other benefits—they allow us to create spaces that cultivate peace, joy, and connection, create spaces for magical work, and spaces to commune with the land. Ask yourself: is this a good time to create, re-think, or expand my existing garden? How could I make an existing garden into a sacred garden? How can I create a space that invites life, creates a space for meditation and reflection? Other possibilities are learning container gardening, indoor gardening, seed sprouting, joining a community garden, or tending public or wild areas. Each of us can find ways of connecting with green, growing things, and making this a regular part of our spiritual practice.

Sacred Actions at Lughnassadh is all about connecting with the green around you and becoming a tender of that land. For those that are looking to convert lawns into gardens or expand existing gardens, the beginning of Fall is a perfect time to start planning for a garden for the coming year in temperate climates. A simple sheet mulched garden bed started in the fall includes using a garden fork to aerate the lawn area, adding a thick layer of cardboard, and layering various organic matter: finished compost, fall leaves, straw, garden waste (weed free—if it has weeds, put it below the cardboard). During winter, these layers will break down into a rich soil that is ready to plant in the spring.

If you do not have land of your own, you can look to wildtending practices: tending the wild areas by scattering seeds in the fall, planting roots, and engaging in other healing-based work. As native plants like common milkweed go to seed, gather these seeds up and on fall walks, scatter them into new areas. These and other simple wildtending activities can help bring healing and care back to our lands.

Learning how to grow plants and tend the lands around you can become an important part of your spiritual practice. You can gain much spiritual insight from observing a seed sprout and grow and tending that plant to harvest. You can create an entirely yearly cycle of activities around your garden, just as our ancient ancestors did, with rituals and activities for planting, growth, and harvest, creating blessings, making offerings, and creating sacred foods from what you have grown.

Prompts for Meditation and Journaling

1. Think back to a time that you visited a garden that impacted you. What was that garden like? What made it so special?

2. Consider that same garden from a sensory perspective. How did you experience it through each of your five senses? What did you sense on a metaphysical or intuitive level?

3. Think about your immediate surroundings: the buildings, houses, streets, and open spaces. If you could transition them into sacred gardens, what would they look like? What kind of work would it take to do this?

4. How has your relationship to nature and the outdoors changed throughout your life?

5. A key aspect of sacred gardening is building a connection with plants. How do you seek connection with the green? What do you consider to be your most sacred plant connection?

6. What is your favorite plant and why? How might this plant be brought into your sacred action practice?

7. What is your favorite outdoor place? Describe it in detail.

8. Many aspects of nature include sacred geometry: the pentacle in the rose petals, the spiral in the unfurling fern frond, the fractal pattern in a Romanesco broccoli. Reflect on some of the most meaningful sacred patterns you have seen in a garden (consider the "art journal" approach below for this entry!).

9. If you could grow anything, what would it be and why?

10. Reflect on your earliest memory in a garden. Where was it? What did you experience? How did you feel?

11. Sacred gardening also involves tending wild spaces—these might be abandoned spaces or those in your local park. Is there a wild space you want to tend? What is your vision for this space?

12. Imagine your perfect sacred garden—a place where you could grow food, plants for spiritual use, support pollinators, and engage in sacred practices. What would this garden look like? (You might use some of the art journaling techniques shared in this chapter to help!)

13. What makes a garden a sacred garden?

14. Consider your best "harvest" experience. What was it? How did it make you feel?

15. What do you see as a care-oriented gardening practice?

Sacred Actions: Experiences and Activities

1. Spend some time with a flower or plant, observing it closely, and connecting to it deeply. If you want to see it up close, consider using a jeweler's loupe to allow you to see close-up detail. What did you learn from this experience?

2. Visit a sacred garden and give yourself enough time (quiet, alone time) to engage in a spiritual practice.

3. Start a seed that you can plant and harvest. Observe the changes to the seed daily and record your experience.

4. Find a way to participate in a harvest: visit a you-pick farm or help out at a community garden or friend's garden. What did you take from this experience?

5. Attend a community harvest festival or food-focused fair. Consider how the harvest is honored through this activity.

6. Build a shrine in an existing garden or area that you cultivate. Consider carefully what the purpose of your shrine is (e.g., veneration, land blessing).

7. Find an abandoned piece of land and do some wildtending and/or energetic work for the space. How does this experience deepen your connection to the land?

Journaling Strategy: Visual and Art Journaling

Art journaling or visual journaling is a journaling technique that combines visual arts (photography, drawing, painting, digital art, collage, mixed media, lettering) with the written word. You don't have to have artistic skills to add visual elements to your journal. Nearly all of the prompts for this season's journaling can include a visual element and may be enhanced if you do so. Some art journal techniques that are accessible to anyone include:

» *Stamping or stenciling.* Find stamps or stencils you like and use them to enhance your journal. Look online or locally for pagan-themed and nature-themed stamps. You can purchase an ink pad or even learn how to make your own ink from plants you grow!

» *Lettering.* Learning how to create interesting lettering can be as simple as investing in a few larger calligraphy pens and markers of various sizes. You can vary the size, shape, and color of your lettering (making certain words or themes emphasized). Be aware that some markers can bleed through pages.

» *Photography.* Take pictures, get them printed, and paste them into your journal. A glue stick or scrapbooking tabs are quite useful for adding these images to your journal and won't warp the pages.

» *Collage.* Save magazines or mailers that come to your home for your journal. When you want to do an entry, search through old magazines to find words, phrases, images, and letters that can enhance your journal. A glue stick works well for this purpose.

» *Drawing and doodling.* Drawings can be simple and still convey meaning. As you practice drawing, your drawing will improve. You can also acquire drawing aids to help you. These aids include a compass, circle sheet, and T-square: these three tools can allow you to make many different patterns.

» *Creative sigil work.* Just as we can free write with the written word (see Ch. 2 Imbloc), you can also free draw and add these to your journal. While there are many kinds of sigils, or symbols used for magical and meditative practice, you can create simple ones by allowing your subconscious to flow forth. This is a channeled technique where you close your eyes and meditate on a theme (such as one of our themes in this season). Now, open your eyes, and draw freely. Don't worry about what your drawing looks like, just allow the theme to come through you. Keep layering (including layering different colors) until you have a symbol or image that speaks to you. This technique can require some practice, but once you have the hang of it, it can powerfully enhance your journaling and magical work.

» *Watercolor wash.* Using a journal designed for mixed media or watercolors (with thicker pages than standard journals), you can do a simple watercolor wash to add interest to your journal. Wet both your page and the watercolors, then drip, brush, and splatter colors onto the page.

» *Leaf rubbing.* Gather up leaves with good veins. Place the leaf under the page and the rub a pencil over the leaf to have a pattern emerge. You can do multiple rubbings with different colored pencils for a layered effect.

CHAPTER 7

Fall Equinox: Earth Ambassadorship, Community, and Broader Work in the World

While much of the Sacred Actions Wheel of the Year is focused on our own lives, at the Fall Equinox, we consider bringing that balance through sacred actions into the broader world. This includes our workplaces, our local communities, and our circles of friends and family. Sacred Actions at the Fall Equinox focuses on how we can make meaningful change in the broader world around us. Earth Ambassadorship is one such philosophy—the idea here is that you speak on behalf of the earth and for the earth, sharing care-oriented philosophies that give voice and agency to the living earth. Earth Ambassadors focus on learning as much as possible about their local landscape, learning how to share that information, and working to reconnect others with nature. There's lots of different approaches to earth ambassadorship, but it is something that each of us can do if we feel that this is a good direction for our paths. Part of connecting people with their local environment and the work of earth ambassadorship could be creating community groups for sharing, knowledge-building, and connection. These might be in the form of sustainability groups, permaculture meetups, community potlucks, community gardens, and other ways to help bring people together to share knowledge of how to heal and sustain the earth. Or, we might work towards something more grand, such as establishing a co-housing or intentional community.

Sacred Action at the Fall Equinox may also include any sustainable activity that we bring to our workplaces—encouraging our workplaces to step up recycling and reducing one-use products, creating gardens or composting systems, and taking the lead in helping our workplaces engage in earth-based decisions. Sacred action at this time can also mean considering our relationship with transportation and its impact on the planet. Can we choose to live somewhere we can walk, bike, or take public transportation? Can we find alternatives to fossil fuels for longer trips? All of these are wonderful ways of building sacred action—and balance—into our broader lives and into our communities.

Prompts for Meditation and Journaling

1. Using the "visioning" journal strategy in this chapter, create a future vision for a healthy, earth-honoring community where you live. What would this community look like?

2. If you have a workplace, consider the same question from the perspective of your workplace. What does your vision for a healthy, earth-honoring workplace look like?

3. For either of these, reflect on steps you might take now and in the future, to make those visions become a reality.

4. Reflect on the theme of balance as it relates to sacred action in your own life and in your community. What does this mean to you?

5. Meditate on the principle of the Earth Ambassador. What does this mean to you? Does it appeal to you? Why or why not?

6. How might you become an Earth Ambassador for your local region? Use Mindmapping (Beltane) or Flow Writing (Summer Solstice) to explore this concept.

7. Write your future vision of you as an Earth Ambassador, five or ten years from now. What do you know? What do you do? What vision are you bringing to the world?

8. One philosophy of fossil fuels is that it is the blood of the earth. If you think about fossil fuel transport from this perspective, how does it change your relationship to fossil-fuel based transportation?

9. Given the challenges we face at present on our planet, it can be hard to focus on the positive. Create a list of at least 10 positive things that are happening in your community or region that are tied to earth care, people care, or fair share. Reflect on what creating this list made you feel.

10. How can broader work in the world be part of your own spiritual practice? What might that offer you?

Sacred Actions: Experiences and Activities

1. Invite friends or family over for a community potluck. Invite people into creative brainstorming for the kinds of things they would like to see in their community and see what comes of your experience.

2. If possible, experiment with an alternative transportation method. What did you get from this experience?

3. If possible, visit an intentional community, co-housing experience, tiny house community or other alternative living arrangement. What did you learn from this experience that you can bring into your own life?

4. Create a "sustainability group" at your workplace or place where you volunteer if one does not exist already and consider direct actions you can engage in to make your workplace/volunteer place more sustainable.

5. Make a list of local and regional organizations that are already engaging in earth care, people care, and or/fair share. Do any of them appeal to you? If so, consider joining an organization and volunteering.

Journaling Strategy:
Visioning the Future Journaling

A big part of the work of Sacred Actions is acting in a care-oriented, sacred manner now so that we can ensure a healthy, healed world for future generations. Through our actions and intentions we are creating the world we want to live in and the world we want to create for the future. This work helps us become good ancestors for future generations. Part of that work is our actions in our world, which allow us to change and shape our physical reality. But another part of that work is by shaping our intentions and working magic—the direction of our own will—through visioning. Thus, one sacred journaling practice allows us to envision the future through creative storytelling. A visioning journaling practice allows us to share a vision for our futures, for our world, and in our paths in getting there. The basic practice is simple: write a hopeful vision of the future and share that vision as widely as you can. Here are some specific strategies:

» *Consider writing stories about your future—what you will do, where you will go, and the work you will accomplish in the world.* These are hopeful, future stories that will help you make your vision a reality.

» *Choose the youngest person in your family.* Write about them and their lives, what they will accomplish, what joy they will bring to the world.

» *Choose to write about the future of your community and how life might be better in 25, 50, or 100 years.*

» *Choose to write the future story of a species that was saved through the care-oriented work of people in your community.*

» *Write a broader vision of the future—write about the success humanity has in solving some of the deep crises of our age, write about the turn towards nature, or write about anything else you would love to see happen.* That is, write what you want to see happen in our world.

» *Once you've written any of the above, consider how you can take actionable steps to get there.* What does the path of sacred action look like in helping you achieve that which you are visioning now?

» *Share your visions with others.* Stories of a hopeful future are so needed now and need to be voiced and shared. Giving voice to a positive future rather than a challenged one is one form of magic we can work in the world.

CHAPTER 8

Samhain: Sustainable Ritual Tools, Items, and Offerings

In the Sacred Actions Wheel of the year, Samhain is time when we focus on the sacred and spiritual work we do. Spiritual tools: sacred objects, ritual items, clothing, stones, and icons all form an important link with our spiritual paths. Thus, in aligning with sustainable, nature-based spiritual practices, at Samhain, we turn to our working tools to see how we can ethically source, use, and draw from materials on our landscape. This is particularly important because our tools carry their own energy—and ethically sourced and used tools will allow us to draw upon that energy to be of benefit to the work we are accomplishing in the world. We can consider this approach from at least three perspectives: developing local, sustainable plant relationships; exploring sustainable ritual tools, clothing, and objects; and developing a deep gratitude and offering practice to ensure reciprocation between what we take from the earth and what we give.

Plants and cultivating plant relationships form the first part of this sustainable tool triad. Some plants—often the most commonly sold in metaphysical shops—have been significantly overharvested and often culturally appropriated (such as Palo Santo, White Sage, Sandalwood, and Frankincense). Many of these plants are now critically endangered and threatened. Thus, we can work to find local, sustainable alternatives—alternatives that we grow or harvest ourselves or that we purchase from ethical growers. For example, most conifer resins in the Pine or Spruce (*Pinacea* spp.) family have resins and needles that are easy to harvest and turn into incense or smoke clearing sticks. Taking time to learn about these different plants and cultivate meaningful relationships with them allows us to grow in our own connection to the living earth and our own practice.

A second area we can consider in terms of sacred action are the ways we source other kinds of tools: candles, clothing, stones, and other ritual objects. Can we find many of our tools out in nature, and harvest them ethically, returning them to the land when we are finished with them? Can we find ways of ethically sourcing clothing for ritual purposes that has been lovingly crafted and ethically harvested/ grown? Can we learn how to repurpose second-hand or other tools for our spiritual use? The idea here is to get our minds into the practice of Sacred Action and see how it can apply to every aspect of our spiritual practice.

A final area of consideration for Sacred Actions as they apply to our spiritual practices is all about gratitude and reciprocation. Offerings are a common practice within neo-paganism, where the idea is that we offer something in exchange for the blessings or gifts we have received or will receive. Considering aspects of sustainable action here, we might think about how we can create offerings that are earth-honoring and sacred. One option is working to make handmade or home-grown offerings such as baking, growing and mixing an offering blend, or creating other small natural crafts. The second is making offerings of your time and energy—going out and planting seeds, cleaning up trash on the landscape, or volunteering in conservation is one of the best offerings one can make. Gifts of the body, such as your own liquid gold or even offering the gift of breath to a tree can also be a sustainable exchange. All of these offering practices can help us develop a greater sense of deep gratitude for the world around us. Through these practices, we can build in new, deeper ways of interacting with the seen and unseen worlds in harmony and respect.

Prompts for Meditation and Journaling

1. What is your favorite ritual tool? How did you come by this tool? Why is it meaningful to you?
2. What does gratitude mean to you? How do you enact it in your life?
3. What does it mean to make an offering? How do you make offerings? Do you have ideas for deepening your offering practice over time?
4. What are common spiritual tools that you use regularly (e.g., incense, candles, etc.)? Is there a possibility of replacing them with more ethically or locally sourced options?
5. Do you have plants that are sacred to you? Why are they sacred to you? What do you do to cultivate a connection with them?
6. What sacred tools would you like to have for your practice?
7. What is the role of your sacred tools—objects, clothing, stones, etc.—in your spiritual practice?
8. Where might you go to find ritual tools, objects, and materials for use in your spiritual practice from local sources or local artisans?
9. Consider the energy of something that you've made yourself vs. the energy of something that you purchased. What is the difference? Can you sense it?
10. Consider the tools of nature—sticks, stones, leaves, shells, and more. How might you deepen your practice with these tools?

Sacred Actions: Experiences and Activities

1. Spend some time finding the local pine species on your landscape (pines, spruces, hemlocks, etc.) and getting to know those plants. Would they be appropriate for use in your spiritual practice?
2. Visit a wild place and give yourself enough time (quiet, alone time) to engage in a ritual, using only tools and materials that you find at that place to build an altar, call the elements, or engage in other ritual practices.
3. Go outside and build a small shrine or nature altar using only what you find. Reflect on this experience and the joy of working together with nature.
4. Growing your own sacred spiritual tools is one path to sacred action. Think about one spiritual tool you use often (e.g., sage to smoke cleanse, a special tea) and reflect on how you might grow it yourself, gather it locally, or replace it with something different that can be locally grown or harvested.
5. Learn to make your own incense from local herbs or your own smoke clearing sticks from local plants. Consider inviting some friends.
6. Take time to cultivate deep gratitude for that which is around you. What does leveling up your gratitude practice look like?
7. Make an offering of your body to a plant or tree. Consider how this experience is different or similar to other offering practices you may have done in the past.

Journaling Strategy: Reflection and Pattern Journaling

As we complete our wheel of the year at Samhain, we return to the themes that began our journaling practice: themes of storytelling, reflection, and deep learning. As we explored at the Winter Solstice, all journaling is a form of written storytelling, where we tell the story of the present to our future selves. This gives us a powerful opportunity to look back on our journal entries over time, reflecting on our own growth and seeing larger patterns and themes in our work. This technique can be done with any of your journals, not only this one, and can lead you into deep insights about the nature of yourself and your path. Here are two possible practices for how you can use reflection.

The first practice is an end-of-journal reflection. This is done when you have filled your previous journal and are ready to start a new one. After you've penned the last few entries of your journal, take a pause and allow a few days for you to re-read the entire journal and reflect. To do this, read through the entries in the journal from cover to cover, and keep a notebook or new journal as you do this. Jot down any insights you have (see the list below for specific suggestions).

You can also take this practice a bit further at key moments in your spiritual path and reflect on all of your spiritual journals over a period of time. For example, I have found it extremely useful to reflect upon my complete spiritual journey, re-reading all of my spiritual journals that I kept over time. I don't do this larger review often, but I do every 5 or so years. I usually do this when I have set aside some time for spiritual retreat and use this as a way of reflecting upon where I've been and where I would like to go next. As you reflect on your journals, you can consider the following questions:

» *What patterns do you see in your experience over time? That is, what are the themes that arise over time?*
» *What are the major areas of growth that you see in your journaling in the last year or more? What have you learned from this experience?*
» *How do the major patterns change as you read? If they do not change, do you consider that a positive thing or a negative thing?*
» *What are the major practices or issues you were wrestling with, and how did those things resolve over time?*
» *How do these patterns help you decide what your future path will be? Where are you going next?*

Conclusion

The journey of sacred actions is one of an ever-deepening spiral, allowing you to continue to transform your own relationship with the living earth as the wheel of the year turns. As you continue to explore your own earth-centered, spiritual practices, recognize the joy, connection, and gratitude that these practices provide.